P9-DGW-044

Kansas City, MO Public Library
00001187914858

Kangaroos

Amazing Jumpers

By Lisa M. Herrington

Children's Press®

An Imprint of Scholastic Inc.

Content Consultants
Taylor Hann
Headkeeper, Australia and the Islands

Kelly Vineyard
Senior Curator, Animal Care
Columbus Zoo and Aquarium

Library of Congress Cataloging-in-Publication Data
Names: Herrington, Lisa M., author.
Title: Kangaroos: amazing jumpers/by Lisa M. Herrington.
Description: New York, NY: Children's Press, an imprint of Scholastic Inc., 2020. | Series: Nature's children | Includes index.
Identifiers: LCCN 2019004831| ISBN 9780531229903 (library binding) | ISBN 9780531239124 (paperback)
Subjects: LCSH: Kangaroos—Juvenile literature.
Classification: LCC QL737.M35 H476 2020 | DDC 599.2/22—dc23

Design by Anna Tunick Tabachnik

Creative Direction: Judith E. Christ for Scholastic

Produced by Spooky Cheetah Press

No part of this publication may be reproduced in whole or in part, or stored in a retrieval system,
or transmitted in any form or by any means, electronic, mechanical, photocopying, recording, or otherwise,
without written permission of the publisher. For information regarding permission, write to Scholastic Inc.,
Attention: Permissions Department, Scholastic Inc., 557 Broadway, New York, NY 10012.
© 2020 Scholastic Inc.

All rights reserved. Published in 2020 by Children's Press, an imprint of Scholastic Inc.

Printed in Heshan, China 62

SCHOLASTIC, CHILDREN'S PRESS, NATURE'S CHILDREN™, and associated logos
are trademarks and/or registered trademarks of Scholastic Inc.

1 2 3 4 5 6 7 8 9 10 R 29 28 27 26 25 24 23 22 21 20

Scholastic Inc., 557 Broadway, New York, NY 10012.

Photographs ©: cover: Freder/iStockphoto; 1: bradleyblackburn/iStockphoto; 4 top: Jim McMahon/Mapman®; 4, leaf silo and throughout: stockgraphicdesigns.com; 5 girl silo: Nowik Sylwia/Shutterstock; 5 rat kangaroo silo: Parer & Parer-Cook/Minden Pictures/age fotostock; 5 kangaroo silo: VKA/Shutterstock; 5 bottom: newboy112/iStockphoto; 6 kangaroo silo and throughout: taeya18/iStockphoto; 7: Dallas Kilponen/The Sydney Morning Herald/Fairfax Media/Getty Images; 8-9: JohnCarnemolla/iStockphoto; 10-11: Saskia Nerlich/Getty Images; 12-13: Smileus/iStockphoto; 14-15: Tier Und Naturfotografie J und C Sohns/Getty Images; 17: Jochen Schlenker/Getty Images; 18-19: Jean-Paul Ferrero/Mary Evans Picture Library Ltd/Agefotostock; 20-21: Parer & Parer-Cook/Minden Pictures/age fotostock; 22-23: Auscape/Getty Images; 25: Martin Harvey/Getty Images; 26-27: Roland Seitre/Minden Pictures/age fotostock; 28-29: Chris Stenger/Buiten-beeld/Minden Pictures; 30-31: Tom McHugh/Science Source; 32-33: David & Micha Sheldon/Getty Images; 35: John Borthwick/Getty Images; 36 top left: Roland Seitre/Minden Pictures/age fotostock; 36 top right: Jiri Lochman/NPL/Minden Pictures; 36 bottom left: Nigel Killeen/Getty Images; 36 bottom right: Tim Graham/Getty Images; 39: Lee Torrens/Shutterstock; 40-41: CB2/ZOB/Supplied by WENN/Newscom; 42 left: Benny Marty/Shutterstock; 42 center: David & Micha Sheldon/mauritius images/age fotostock; 42 left: Martin Willis/Minden Pictures/age footstock; 43 top center: Pete Oxford/NPL/Minden Pictures; 43 top right: Parer & Parer-Cook/Minden Pictures/age fotostock; 43 right: Joel Sartore/Getty Images; 43 bottom center: Eric Isselee/Biosphoto/Alamy Images; 46: David & Micha Sheldon/mauritius images/age fotostock.

◀ **Cover image shows a red kangaroo in mid-hop!**

Table of Contents

Fact File...4

CHAPTER 1   **Large Leapers**..6
       Meet These Hoppers......................................9
       Home, Sweet Home.......................................10
       Built to Bounce..13
       Hopping to It..14

CHAPTER 2   **A Mob Scene**..16
       Danger from Dingoes....................................19
       Chew on This!...20
       Keeping Cool...23

CHAPTER 3   **Starting a Family**...24
       Pouch Babies...26
       Roo Rider...29
       Growing Up and Out.....................................30
       Off into the World..33

CHAPTER 4   **Monster Marsupials**....................................34
       Meet the Relatives..37

CHAPTER 5   **Australia's Symbol**......................................38
       Rescuing Roos...40

Kangaroo Family Tree..42
Words to Know...44
Find Out More..46
Index..47
About the Author...48

Fact File: Kangaroos

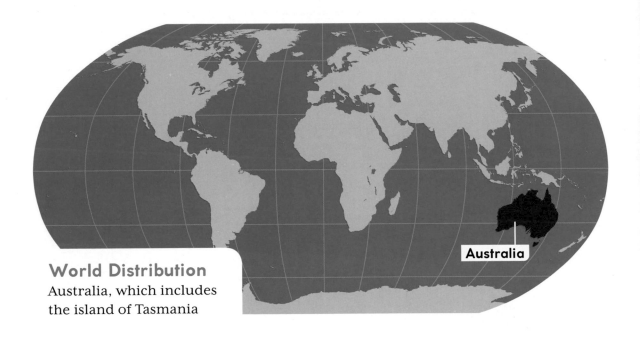

World Distribution
Australia, which includes
the island of Tasmania

Australia

Habitat
A variety of
environments,
including grassy
plains, deserts,
and woodlands

Habits
Fast, powerful
hoppers; live
mostly in groups;
generally rest in
the shade during
the day and eat at
night; males box
over females

Diet
Plants, grasses,
leaves, roots,
and flowers

**Distinctive
Features**
Bodies covered in
fur; powerful hind
legs and large feet;
enlarged muscular
tail; females carry
babies in pouches

Fast Fact
Kangaroos are
called "roos"
for short.

Average Size

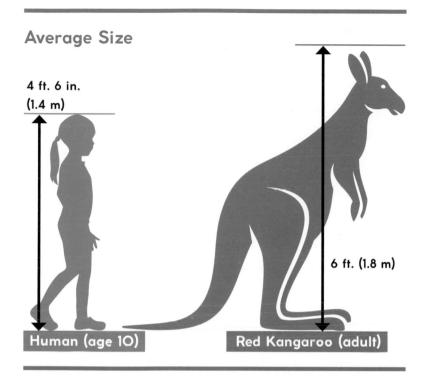

4 ft. 6 in.
(1.4 m)

Human (age 10)

6 ft. (1.8 m)

Red Kangaroo (adult)

Classification

CLASS
Mammalia (mammals)

ORDER
Diprotodontia
(kangaroos, wallabies,
opossums, koalas,
wombats, and
relatives)

FAMILY
Macropodidae

GENUS
Macropus

SPECIES
- *Macropus rufus*
  (red kangaroo)
- *Macropus giganteus*
  (eastern gray
  kangaroo)
- *Macropus fuliginosus*
  (western gray
  kangaroo)
- *Macropus antilopinus*
  (antilopine kangaroo)

◄ When standing,
a kangaroo leans on
its tail for support.

CHAPTER 1

Large Leapers

The late-afternoon sun casts a warm glow over Australia's **plains**. A group of kangaroos hop about, nibbling on grass. A baby kangaroo peeks its head out of its mother's cozy pouch. Then it quickly ducks back in. For now, the baby is content to enjoy the ride.

Suddenly, a strange noise nearby startles the kangaroos. Their tall ears perk up. The sound may be from a pack of wild dogs, but the kangaroos aren't sticking around to find out. Springing into action, the kangaroos begin to bounce—faster and faster—scattering in different directions. They can leap the length of a school bus in one bound, leaving danger in their dust.

Kangaroos are the only large animals that hop to move, and they are among the world's best jumpers. Their remarkable leaping ability, unusual body shape, and adorable pouch babies make them some of the most fascinating animals on Earth.

▶ A group of kangaroos make a quick getaway when danger is near.

Meet These Hoppers

When we think of kangaroos, the four largest **species** typically come to mind. They are the red kangaroo, the eastern gray kangaroo, the western gray kangaroo, and the antilopine kangaroo. These are the species we describe in this book.

However, the family to which these kangaroos belong includes many smaller species such as wallaroos, wallabies, and quokkas. There are more than 50 species in the family! Learn more about them on page 37.

The red kangaroo is the biggest species. It can grow to about 6 feet (1.8 meters) tall and weigh up to 200 pounds (90.7 kilograms). Eastern and western gray kangaroos are almost as tall but are not as heavy. They all have big feet that can grow to 18 inches (45.7 centimeters) long.

All these large kangaroos belong to a group of **mammals** called **marsupials**. Most female marsupials have pouches on their bellies to carry and feed their young. Baby marsupials do most of their developing inside their mother's pouch.

◄ The red kangaroo is the world's largest marsupial.

Home, Sweet Home

Large kangaroos live in mainland Australia and Tasmania. They are found in a wide variety of environments, from grasslands to deserts to sandy shores. Different species of large kangaroos live in different **habitats**. Red kangaroos make their home in remote wilderness areas of central Australia known as the **outback**. They mostly like to bounce across its hot, dry open plains and deserts. Few trees grow in these inland areas, and there is little water.

Gray kangaroos prefer the woodlands and **bushland** of eastern, western, and southern Australia. These areas get more rain. The kangaroos that live there are nicknamed "foresters" because they are found where there are more trees. They move to areas of open grasslands when they **graze**. Antilopine kangaroos can be found in Australia's northern woodlands.

▶ These eastern gray kangaroos relax on a sandy beach in Australia.

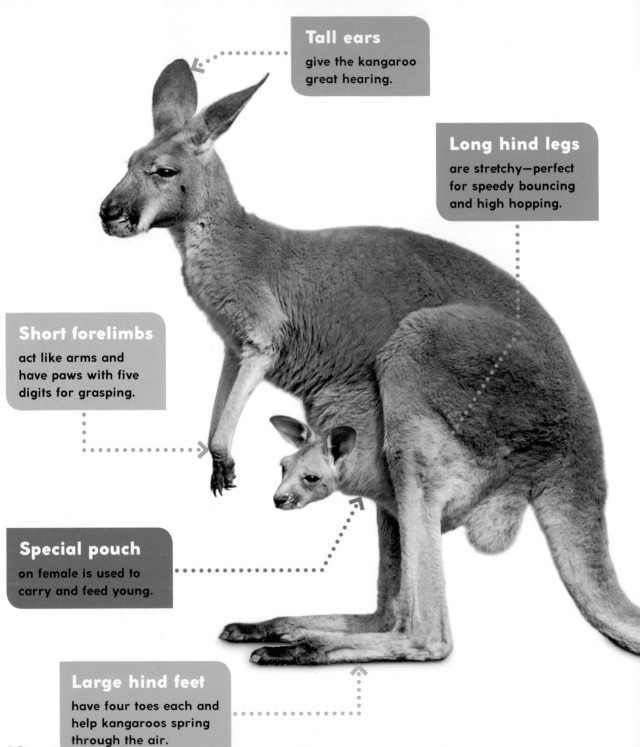

Tall ears give the kangaroo great hearing.

Long hind legs are stretchy—perfect for speedy bouncing and high hopping.

Short forelimbs act like arms and have paws with five digits for grasping.

Special pouch on female is used to carry and feed young.

Large hind feet have four toes each and help kangaroos spring through the air.

Built to Bounce

Kangaroos have tall ears, a long face, two strong back legs, two short forelimbs, and a big tail. Their front paws can be used for grasping plants, scratching themselves, and **grooming** their fur.

Most kangaroos have gray or brown fur, but their color can vary by species and even **gender**. Male red kangaroos, for example, tend to have red fur, but females of the same species are gray or even bluish.

To find food, kangaroos cover long distances. And they do it by hopping! A large kangaroo's body is designed for jumping. Along with powerful hind legs and huge feet, these kangaroos rely on their tails for leaping. A kangaroo's tail can grow to 4 feet (1.2 meters) long and helps the animal balance and steer. The tail acts as a **rudder** when the kangaroo wants to change direction.

Muscular tail
provides balance for jumping and support for standing.

Hopping to It

You might already know that kangaroos are jumping machines, but would you believe they can travel as fast as a car? Large kangaroos can leap at speeds of 30 miles (48.3 kilometers) per hour. If they need to escape danger, kangaroos can exceed 40 mph (64.4 kph).

As they move, kangaroos tuck in their forelimbs and bounce on both of their strong hind legs at the same time. Their legs are made up of tough, flexible **tendons** that attach muscles to bones. They work like springs. A kangaroo's legs tighten when the animal lands and expand when it jumps. As a kangaroo hops forward, its long tail swings up and down. This super jumper can leap more than 30 ft. (9.1 m) in a single hop!

When kangaroos move slowly to graze, they arch their bodies and crawl-walk on all fours. To do this, they lean over so that their front legs and their tail are on the ground. Then they swing their back legs forward.

▶ Kangaroos are among the world's highest-jumping animals.

Fast Fact

Kangaroos must
move their legs
together to jump.

CHAPTER 2

A Mob Scene

Kangaroos tend to be social animals.

Most large kangaroos live in groups called **mobs**. These groups can be made up of anywhere from three to 50 or more kangaroos.

Male kangaroos are called bucks or boomers. The largest and strongest male in the group usually becomes the mob's leader. The mob's females are called does or flyers. Since they are much lighter and smaller than males, they can hop faster. They move quickly and spend so much time in the air that they look like they are flying!

Kangaroos in mobs like to groom each other. They use their front paws to pick dirt and small insects off each other.

Kangaroos make noises to communicate. They may bark, cough, or growl if they feel threatened. Mothers make clicking or clucking sounds—usually several times in a row—to call their young. Kangaroos also touch noses to say hello.

▶ A mob of eastern gray kangaroos stand alert to danger.

Fast Fact
Kangaroos are
unable to hop
backward.

Danger from Dingoes

Large kangaroos don't have many enemies. Their main **predators** are wild dogs called dingoes. Young kangaroos face threats from foxes and eagles.

Living in a group helps keep kangaroos safe. The more animals checking for threats, the better. Kangaroos use their excellent hearing to listen closely for danger while other members of the group are eating or sleeping.

When a kangaroo is alert, it stands tall and looks out for trouble. If danger is near, kangaroos stomp their feet loudly to warn others. The members of the mob then dart away in different directions.

To protect itself, a kangaroo can kick an enemy with a dangerous weapon—its powerful hind legs. Its toes also have deadly sharp claws.

Kangaroos are good swimmers and may even go into water to make a quick getaway. Unfortunately, escape is not always possible.

◀ A pack of dingoes works together to hunt a kangaroo.

Chew on This!

Kangaroos are **herbivores**. That means they mainly feed on plants. Different species munch on different kinds of grasses, leaves, and flowers.

A kangaroo's sharp front teeth, called **incisors**, work like scissors, snipping grasses and leaves. Broad, flat back teeth called **molars** crush and grind the tough food. Because kangaroos chew so much, their molars often wear down completely. In some species, the worn-down teeth are replaced with new molars that move forward.

Some grasses are difficult to digest. So kangaroos **regurgitate**, or cough up, their food and chew it again, as cows and sheep do. Bacteria in the kangaroo's stomach help break down the food.

While eating, kangaroos may rest on their back legs. As a mother grazes, her baby, called a **joey**, may also lean out of the pouch to eat.

Kangaroos need water, but they can go long stretches without it. They can live on almost as little water as camels do. They get a lot of their water from the plants they eat.

▶ Kangaroos spend seven to 14 hours a day eating.

Fast Fact
Kangaroos like
to sleep on
their sides.

Keeping Cool

Many kangaroos eat when it is cooler. The animals start moving around in the early evening and stay active until dawn. During the day kangaroos try to rest in shady spots to avoid overheating out in the open plains and grasslands. But it can be hard to find shade in areas with few trees. So red kangaroos, for example, dig holes in the ground to make cool places where they can rest and seek refuge from the sun. They scrape away the hot **topsoil** to get to the cooler ground below.

Licking their forearms is another way that kangaroos keep cool. They have less hair on this part of their body. As the wet saliva dries, it cools the kangaroos' blood and lowers their body temperature.

◀ These red kangaroos have dug shallow holes near bushes to try to stay cool.

23

CHAPTER 3

Starting a Family

Male kangaroos can become fierce and competitive. Sometimes they wrestle over a shady resting spot or even over water. But they mainly fight to win a female.

When males fight, they use their short forearms to box and jab. They use their front paws for pushing and punching. They also swat each other in the face or chest.

A kangaroo's huge hind feet can deliver powerful blows. The animals kick each other with their clawed feet. A fight usually ends when one of the kangaroos gives up and hops away. The winner is the **dominant** male. He will **mate** with most of the mob's females. He usually becomes the father of almost all the mob's joeys. When a female is ready to mate, the dominant male will follow her.

▶ As kangaroos box, they throw their heads back to protect their eyes and ears.

Pouch Babies

About five weeks after mating, the mother kangaroo gives birth to a very tiny baby. The newborn kangaroo is no bigger than a jelly bean and weighs about 0.04 ounces (1.1 grams)! The baby is only partly developed. It doesn't have hair and can't see.

Like all marsupials, the baby spends less time growing in its mother's body than other mammals do. For example, a human baby spends 40 weeks in its mother's belly and usually weighs 5 to 8 pounds (2.3 to 3.6 kilograms) at birth.

Despite its miniature size, the newborn kangaroo grips its mother's fur with its short front limbs and crawls its way into her pouch. The journey takes about five minutes.

Once inside, the newborn begins nursing from one of its mother's four nipples. The nipple swells to fill the newborn's mouth so the baby stays firmly attached to its mother. The pouch offers food, shelter, and protection for the baby so it can grow and finish developing.

▶ This newborn red kangaroo joey hardly looks like a kangaroo at all!

Fast Fact
Females raise joeys without help from the male.

Roo Rider

It takes a while for the baby to get fur and begin to look like a kangaroo. By four or five months old, the joey pops its head out for the first time. It's about the size of a cat.

When the joey has to go to the bathroom, it does so right inside the pouch. The pouch's lining absorbs some of the **waste**, but the mother also licks her pouch clean. She also regularly pokes her head inside to groom her baby.

When it's time to bounce, the mother kangaroo buckles her jocy in for the ride. She does this by tightening the muscles at the top of her pouch so her baby can't fall out.

The joey will remain in the pouch until it is about eight months old. Then it climbs out to explore the world for short periods of time. A joey's early hops are wobbly, but they eventually become stronger.

When the joey becomes frightened or tired and wants to return to the pouch, the mother relaxes the opening. The joey will dive back into the pouch—headfirst. Inside the pouch, the baby kangaroo does a somersault to turn itself around so its head is near the opening.

◀ A western gray kangaroo nuzzles her joey.

Growing Up and Out

As it grows, the baby kangaroo spends more time outside its mother's pouch. Before long it becomes too big for the pouch. At nine to 12 months, depending on the species, the joey leaves the pouch for good. It is also called a young-at-foot now.

The young-at-foot still relies on its mother. It may even try to get back into its mother's pouch, but she won't let it. She licks her pouch clean and prepares it for a new brother or sister to arrive.

A mother can have three babies with her at once—all at different stages. She may have a newborn snug in her pouch, with the young-at-foot at her side. The third baby is inside her body, waiting to be born once the joey leaves her pouch.

▶ This young-at-foot is adjusting to life outside its mother's pouch.

Off into the World

A mother kangaroo nurses the new baby and her young-at-foot at the same time. She can produce two different kinds of milk—one tailored for the joey in her pouch and one for the young kangaroo next to her. While occasionally sticking its head back into the pouch to nurse, the young-at-foot also eats grasses and plants. It continues to nurse until it is 12 to 18 months old.

Young kangaroos like to playfully box. Mothers also practice boxing with their joeys to teach them how to defend themselves. By the time they are two to three years old, young kangaroos have become independent.

Females are ready to have babies when they are about two years old. Some stay near their mothers after they have their own joeys. Males are ready to mate when they are around 2 years old. They may start a new mob or join another group of kangaroos.

In the wild, kangaroos live six to eight years. In zoos, they can live to be about 20 years old.

◀ Kangaroos still nurse for several months after they leave the pouch.

CHAPTER 4

Monster Marsupials

No one knows for sure how today's kangaroos developed. But scientists think the first tiny marsupial **ancestors** most likely developed millions of years ago in what is now North America, and then spread to South America, Antarctica, and Australia. At that time, these continents were connected. But little by little, Australia began to separate. It became its own landmass about 80 million years ago.

Scientists think monster-sized marsupials evolved in Australia about 13 million years ago. They included a kangaroo that stood 10 ft. (3 m) high. Because of their enormous size, these roos likely walked instead of hopped. They became **extinct** about 30,000 years ago. Today's kangaroos may have **descended** from these giant animals.

▶ **This cave art from thousands of years ago shows a kangaroo and a hunter.**

Tree Kangaroo

▶ This tree kangaroo uses its curved claws and strong arms for climbing.

Rock Wallaby

▶ Some rock wallabies have special soles on their feet so they don't slip on cliffs.

Quokka

These leaf-eating marsupials often look like they are smiling.

Musky Rat Kangaroo

▶ Distant relatives of kangaroos, this species can fit in a person's hand.

Meet the Relatives

The kangaroo family has many members! The largest are simply known as kangaroos.

Then there are wallaroos and wallabics. Wallaroos are smaller than kangaroos, and wallabies are smaller than wallaroos. Both mostly look and act just like their large kangaroo cousins. There are brush, swamp, forest, and rock wallabies. Their names offer clues as to where they are found. Pademelons and quokkas, other small members of the kangaroo family, live in forests.

Fourteen species of tree kangaroos make their home in rain forests in Australia and New Guinea. These mysterious creatures live in trees and are difficult to spot among the branches. Unlike large members of the kangaroo family, they can move their back legs independently of each other.

Potoroos, bettongs, and rat kangaroos are distant relatives of kangaroos. They are also marsupials, but they belong to a different scientific family. Many are **endangered** due to habitat loss and other threats.

◀ Check out some amazing kangaroo relatives.

CHAPTER 5

Australia's Symbol

The kangaroo is Australia's most well-known animal and is one of the country's national symbols. Kangaroos appear on Australia's coat of arms and on some of its currency. Some of the country's sports teams are nicknamed after kangaroos, and these beautiful bouncers are featured on its main airline.

About 50 million large kangaroos live in Australia. That's double the number of people living there! Still, humans can cause a threat. Each year, more than a million kangaroos are killed. Some leap in front of cars. Farmers may hunt kangaroos because they eat grasses meant for cattle and sheep. Because there are so many kangaroos in Australia, it is legal to hunt a certain number each year. Some people hunt kangaroos to make leather from their skin. Others hunt them for their meat. Kangaroo meat is sometimes used as pet food and is also eaten by people.

▶ In Australia, kangaroo crossing signs warn drivers to be careful.

Rescuing Roos

Some kangaroos, including those that are hurt in accidents, live in special places called animal **sanctuaries**. They can't be hunted there and are free to leap and bound over large areas. Tourists can visit the sanctuaries to see these creatures up close.

At the Kangaroo Sanctuary in Alice Springs, Australia, wildlife experts rescue and care for joeys that have lost their mothers. The workers wrap the orphaned babies in warm, cozy pouches made from pillowcases, canvas bags, or blankets. This mimics the safety and comfort of a mother's pouch and gives the joeys room to move.

An animal hospital at this sanctuary helps injured kangaroos. Some of these kangaroos are released back into the wild. Wildlife experts are working hard to ensure that healthy roos are jumping into the future.

▶ Orphaned joeys at the Kangaroo Sanctuary get some snuggle time.

Kangaroo Family Tree

This diagram shows how kangaroos are related to some of their relatives. All these animals are marsupials. That means the females carry their babies in a pouch.

Eastern and Western Gray Kangaroos
large kangaroos that inhabit moist open forests and other habitats

Red Kangaroos
largest kangaroos, which are found on Australia's dry interior plains and grasslands

Wallaroos
medium-sized hoppers that fall between their larger kangaroo cousins and wallabies in size

Wallabies
animals that are smaller than wallaroos and that live in many places, including rocky cliffs

Tree Kangaroos
small kangaroos that climb treetops in Queensland, Australia

Musky Rat Kangaroos
small marsupials, which live in rain forests in northeast Australia

Bettongs
Australia's small, short-nosed marsupials, which are active at night

Ancestor of all Kangaroos

Note: Animal photos are not to scale.

Words to Know

A .... **ancestors** *(ANN-sess-turs)* family members who lived long ago

B .... **bushland** *(BUSH-land)* wooded area with bushes and shrubs and little dense vegetation

D .... **descended** *(di-SEND-ed)* came from an earlier generation of the same family

dominant *(DAH-muh-nuhnt)* most influential or powerful

E .... **endangered** *(en-DAYN-juhrd)* in danger of becoming extinct, usually because of human activity

extinct *(ik-STINGKT)* no longer found alive

G .... **gender** *(JEN-dur)* the male or female sex

graze *(GRAYZ)* to feed on grass that is growing in a field

grooming *(GROOM-ing)* brushing or cleaning

H .... **habitats** *(HAB-i-tats)* the places where an animal or plant is usually found

herbivores *(HUR-buh-vorz)* animals that eat only plants

I .... **incisors** *(in-SYE-zurz)* teeth in the front of the mouth that are used for cutting

J .... **joey** *(JO-ee)* a baby marsupial

M .... **mammals** *(MAM-uhlz)* warm-blooded animals that have hair or fur and usually give birth to live babies; female mammals produce milk to feed their young

marsupials *(mar-SOO-pee-uhls)* animals where the females carry their babies in a pouch on their abdomens

mate *(MAYT)* to join together for breeding

mobs *(MOBS)* groups of kangaroos

molars *(MOH-lurz)* the wide, flat teeth at the back of the mouth used for crushing and chewing food

N .... **nurse** *(NURS)* to feed a baby milk from a breast

O .... **outback** *(out-BAK)* the remote and usually uninhabited regions of inland Australia

P .... **plains** *(PLANES)* large, flat areas of land with few trees

predators *(PRED-uh-tuhrs)* animals that live by hunting other animals for food

R .... **regurgitate** *(ree-GERJ-uh-tayt)* to bring food that has been swallowed back from the stomach into the mouth

rudder *(RUHD-ur)* something used for steering

S .... **sanctuaries** *(SANGK-choo-er-eez)* natural areas where animals are protected from hunters

species *(SPEE-sheez)* one of the groups into which animals and plants are divided; members of the same species can mate and have offspring

T .... **tendons** *(TEN-duhns)* strong, thick cords or bands of tissue that join muscle to bones or other body parts

topsoil *(TAHP-soil)* the top layer of soil that contains the nutrients that plants need to grow

W .... **waste** *(WAYST)* what the body does not use or need after food has been digested

Find Out More

BOOKS

- Bishop, Nic. *Marsupials*. New York: Scholastic, 2009.

- Donohue, Moira Rose. *Kangaroo to the Rescue!: And More True Stories of Amazing Animal Heroes*. Washington, D.C.: National Geographic Kids, 2015.

- Ganeri, Anita. *The Story of the Kangaroo*. Chicago: Capstone, 2016.

- Robbins, Lynette. *Kangaroos* (Jump!). New York: PowerKids Press, 2012.

- Wilsdon, Christina. *Kangaroos* (Amazing Animals). New York: Gareth Stevens Publishing, 2011.

To find more books and resources about animals, visit:

scholastic.com

Index

A

ancestors 34, *35*

antilopine kangaroos 9, 10

Australia 6, 10, 37, 38, *39*, 40

B

babies 26, *27*, *28*, 29, 30, *31*, *32*, 33

boxing *25*, 33

C

cave art 34, *35*

coloring 13

communication 16, 19

conservation efforts 40, *41*

crawl-walking 14

D

diet 6, 10, 20, 26, 33

dingoes *18*, 19

distribution 6, 10, 38, *39*, 40

F

female kangaroos 9, 13, 16, 24, 29, 33

forelimbs *12*, 13, 14

foresters 10

G

grazing 10, 14, 20, *21*, 33

grooming 13, 16, 29

H

habitats 6, 10, *11*, 37

herbivores 20

hopping and jumping 6, *7*, 13, 14, *15*, 16, 19, 29, 34, *39*

K

Kangaroo Sanctuary 40, *41*

keeping cool 22, 23

kicking 19, 24, *25*

L

legs *12*, 13, 14, *15*, 19, 20, 37

lifespan 33

M

male kangaroos 13, 16, 24, *25*, 29, 33

marsupials 9, 26, 34, *36*

mating 24, 26, 33

mobs 16, *17*, 19, 24, 33

Index *(continued)*

N

nursing......................9, 26, *27*, *32*, 33

P

pademelons 37

population size 38

pouches.................6, *8*, 9, *12*, 20, 26, *27*, *28*, 29, *32*, 33

predators...........................6, *18*, 19

R

regurgitation 20

S

sanctuaries 40, *41*

size and weight 9, 26

species of kangaroos 9, 10, 13, 23, *36*, 37

speed..14

T

tails *12*, 13, 14

teeth.. 20

threats.....................6, *18*, 19, 37, 38

Y

young-at-foot kangaroos......... 30, *31*, *32*, 33

About the Author

Lisa M. Herrington has written many books and articles for kids. She loves learning all about different animals, from ferocious wolves to fast-jumping kangaroos. Lisa graduated from Syracuse University and received a master's degree in publishing from New York University. Lisa lives in Trumbull, Connecticut, with her husband, Ryan, and her little roo, Caroline.